Companion to
A Lake Po

Companions of Nature:
A Lake Poets Anthology

Rothay Books

First Published 2019

Contents

Catherine Gilpin (1738-1811)
  Trafalgar Sea-Fight, 1805 — 1

Susanna Blamire (1747-1794)
  The Siller Croun — 3
  Barley Broth — 4

William Wordsworth (1770-1850)
  Resolution and Independence — 6
  My heart leaps up when I behold — 11
  It was an April morning: fresh and clear — 12
  I wandered lonely as a Cloud — 14
  Surprised by Joy — 15
  Sonnets from The River Duddon: After-Thought — 16

Robert Anderson (1770-1833)
  The Cummerlan Farmer — 17

John Stagg (1770-1823)
  The Wolf and the Shepherd — 20

Dorothy Wordsworth (1771-1855)
  Floating Island — 21
  To my Niece Dorothy, a sleepless Baby — 22

Loving and Liking:
   Irregular Verses Addressed to a Child   23
Thoughts on my Sick-bed   26
When shall I tread your garden path...   28

Samuel Taylor Coleridge (1772-1834)
  Dejection: An Ode   29
  To Asra   35
  A Sunset   36
  A Thought Suggested by a View of Saddleback
   in Cumberland   37
  Frost at Midnight   38

Robert Southey (1774-1843)
  from The Poet's Pilgrimage to Waterloo: Proem   41
  Epitaph   43
  Spring   44
  My days among the Dead are Past   45
  The Cataract of Lodore   46

Isabella Lickbarrow (1784-1847)
  On Esthwaite Water   50
  Written in a Cemetery   52

John Wilson (Christopher North) (1785-1854)
  Wastwater in a Storm   54
  Wastwater in a Calm   55

Edward Quillinan (1791-1851)
  The Birch of Silver-How   56

Felicia Hemans (1793-1835)
  A Remembrance of Grasmere   58
  To Wordsworth   59

Hartley Coleridge (1796-1849)
  Dedicatory Sonnet to S.T. Coleridge   61
  Long time a child, and still a child, when years   62
  To A Friend Leaving Grasmere   63
  Lines Written Impromptu After Hearing
    A Lady Singing   64

William Dickinson (1799-1882)
  The Words of Oald Cummerlan'   65

Sara Coleridge (1802-1852)
  The Months   67

Letitia Elizabeth Landon (L.E.L.) (1802-1838)   69
  Coniston Water

John Richardson (1817-1886)
  "It's Nobbut Me!"   70

Edmund Lee (1844-1931)
  To F.H. (By The Wishing-Gate)   72
  In Grasmere Churchyard   74

Catherine Gilpin
(1738-1811)

Trafalgar Sea-Fight, 1805

O lass! I's fit to brust wi' news!
There's letters frae the fleet;
We've bang'd the French, aye, out and out'
An' duin the thing complete:
There was sec show'rs o' shell grenades,
Bunch'd out wi' shot, like grapes;
An' bullets, big as beath our heads,
Chain'd twea an' twea wi' reapes.

Our Jwohn was perch'd abuin the'r heads,
To keep a sharp luik out;
An' tell them, gin he kent his-sel',
What they wer' aw about:
They skimm'd the skin of Jwohnny's cheek,
He niver heeded that,
But rwoar'd, tho' he was main-mast height,
"We'll pay them weel for that!"

It was a seet! our Jwohnny says,
A seet nit often seen;
An' aw the'r colours flifty flaff—
Some reed, some blue, some green:
The French rang'd up in aw the'r pride,
Afwore our thunder brast;
But lang afwore it ceas'd to rwoar,
It hardly left a mast.

But we ha'e paid a fearfu' preyce;
For Nelson is no more!
That soul o' fire has breath'd his last,
Far frae his native shore!
"O waes in me!" our Jwohnny says,
"That I sud ha'e to tell;
"For nit a man aboard the fleet,
"But wish'd t' had been his-sel'."

Our British tars hev kindly hearts,
Tho' you wad hardly ken;
They'll shout, when ships are gangin' down,
But try to seave the men:
They'll risk the life that's hardly won,
To bring them to the shore;
An' sorrow dashes owre their een,
When they can do no more.

Susanna Blamire
(1747-1794)

The Siller Croun

And ye shall walk in silk attire,
And siller hae to spare,
Gin ye'll consent to be his bride,
Nor think o' Donald mair.
O wha wad buy a silken goun
Wi' a poor broken heart!
Or what's to me a siller croun,
Gin frae my love I part!

The mind wha's every wish is pure
Far dearer is to me;
And ere I'm forc'd to break my faith,
I'll lay me down an' dee!
For I ha'e pledged my virgin troth
Brave Donald's fate to share;
And he has gi'en to me his heart,
Wi' a' its virtues rare.

His gentle manners wan my heart,
He gratefu' took the gift;
Could I but think to seek it back,
It wad be waur than theft!
For langest life can ne'er repay
The love he bears to me;
And ere I'm forced to break my troth
I'll lay me doun an' dee.

Susanna Blamire

Barley Broth

If tempers were put up to seale,
Our Jwohn's wad bear a duced preyce;
He vow'd 'twas barley i' the broth,—
Upon my word, says I, it's reyce.

"I mek nea faut," our Jwohnny says,
"The broth is guid and varra neyce;
I only say—it's barley broth."
Tou says what's wrang, says I, it's reyce.

"Did ever mortal hear the leyke!
As if I hadn't sense to tell!
Tou may think reyce the better thing,
But barley broth dis just as well."

"And sae it mud, if it was there;
The deil a grain is i' the pot;
But tou mun ayways threep yen down,—
I've drawn the deevil of a lot!"

"And what's the lot that I have drawn?
Pervarsion is a woman's neame!
Sae fares-te-weel! I'll sarve my king,
And never, never mair come heame."

Now Jenny frets frae mworn to neet;
The Sunday cap's nae langer neyce;
She aye puts barley i' the broth,
And hates the varra neame o' reyce.

Susanna Blamire

Thus treyfles vex, and treyfles please,
And treyfles mek the sum o' leyfe;
And treyfles mek a bonny lass
A wretched or a happy weyfe!

William Wordsworth
(1770–1850)

Resolution and Independence

There was a roaring in the wind all night;
The rain came heavily and fell in floods;
But now the sun is rising calm and bright;
The birds are singing in the distant woods;
Over his own sweet voice the Stock-dove broods;
The Jay makes answer as the Magpie chatters;
And all the air is filled with pleasant noise of waters.

All things that love the sun are out of doors;
The sky rejoices in the morning's birth;
The grass is bright with rain-drops;—on the moors
The hare is running races in her mirth;
And with her feet she from the plashy earth
Raises a mist; which, glittering in the sun,
Runs with her all the way, wherever she doth run.

I was a Traveller then upon the moor;
I saw the hare that raced about with joy;
I heard the woods, and distant waters, roar;
Or heard them not, as happy as a boy:
The pleasant season did my heart employ:
My old remembrances went from me wholly;
And all the ways of men, so vain and melancholy.

But, as it sometimes chanceth, from the might
Of joy in minds that can no further go,
As high as we have mounted in delight

William Wordsworth

In our dejection do we sink as low,
To me that morning did it happen so;
And fears and fancies thick upon me came;
Dim sadness, and blind thoughts I knew not nor
    could name.

I heard the sky-lark singing in the sky;
And I bethought me of the playful hare:
Even such a happy Child of earth am I;
Even as these blissful creatures do I fare;
Far from the world I walk, and from all care;
But there may come another day to me,
Solitude, pain of heart, distress, and poverty.

My whole life I have lived in pleasant thought,
As if life's business were a summer mood;
As if all needful things would come unsought
To genial faith, still rich in genial good;
But how can He expect that others should
Build for him, sow for him, and at his call
Love him, who for himself will take no heed at all?

I thought of Chatterton, the marvellous Boy,
The sleepless Soul that perished in his pride;
Of Him who walked in glory and in joy
Behind his plough, upon the mountain-side:
By our own spirits are we deified:
We Poets in our youth begin in gladness;
But thereof comes in the end despondency and madness.

Now, whether it were by peculiar grace,
A leading from above, a something given,

William Wordsworth

Yet it befel, that, in this lonely place,
When up and down my fancy thus was driven,
And I with these untoward thoughts had striven,
I saw a Man before me unawares:
The oldest man he seemed that ever wore grey hairs.

My course I stopped as soon as I espied
The Old Man in that naked wilderness:
Close by a Pond, upon the further side,
He stood alone: a minute's space I guess
I watched him, he continuing motionless:
To the Pool's further margin then I drew;
He being all the while before me full in view.

As a huge stone is sometimes seen to lie
Couched on the bald top of an eminence;
Wonder to all who do the same espy,
By what means it could thither come, and whence;
So that it seems a thing endued with sense:
Like a sea-beast crawled forth, that on a shelf
Of rock or sand reposeth, there to sun itself;

Such seemed this Man, not all alive nor dead,
Nor all asleep; in his extreme old age:
His body was bent double, feet and head
Coming together in their pilgrimage;
As if some dire constraint of pain, or rage
Of sickness felt by him in times long past,
A more than human weight upon his frame had cast.

Himself he propped, his body, limbs, and face,
Upon a long grey staff of shaven wood:

William Wordsworth

And, still as I drew near with gentle pace,
Beside the little pond or moorish flood
Motionless as a cloud the Old Man stood,
That heareth not the loud winds when they call;
And moveth all together, if it move at all.

At length, himself unsettling, he the Pond
Stirred with his staff, and fixedly did look
Upon the muddy water, which he conned,
As if he had been reading in a book:
And now such freedom as I could I took;
And, drawing to his side, to him did say,
"This morning gives us promise of a glorious day."

A gentle answer did the old Man make,
In courteous speech which forth he slowly drew:
And him with further words I thus bespake,
"What kind of work is that which you pursue?
This is a lonesome place for one like you."
He answered me with pleasure and surprise;
And there was, while we spake, a fire about his eyes.

His words came feebly, from a feeble chest,
But each in solemn order followed each,
With something of a lofty utterance drest;
Choice word, and measured phrase; above the reach
Of ordinary men; a stately speech!
Such as grave Livers do in Scotland use,
Religious men, who give to God and Man their dues.

He told me that he to this pond had come
To gather leeches, being old and poor:

Employment hazardous and wearisome!
And he had many hardships to endure:
From pond to pond he roamed, from moor to moor;
Housing, with God's good help, by choice or chance;
And in this way he gained an honest maintenance.

The Old Man still stood talking by my side;
But now his voice to me was like a stream
Scarce heard; nor word from word could I divide;
And the whole body of the Man did seem
Like one whom I had met with in a dream;
Or like a man from some far region sent,
To give me human strength, and strong admonishment.

My former thoughts returned: the fear that kills;
And hope that is unwilling to be fed;
Cold, pain, and labour, and all fleshly ills;
And mighty Poets in their misery dead.
And now, not knowing what the Old Man had said,
My question eagerly did I renew,
"How is it that you live, and what is it you do?"

He with a smile did then his words repeat;
And said, that, gathering leeches, far and wide
He travelled; stirring thus about his feet
The waters of the pools where they abide.
"Once I could meet with them on every side;
But they have dwindled long by slow decay;
Yet still I persevere, and find them where I may."

While he was talking thus, the lonely place,
The Old Man's shape, and speech, all troubled me:

William Wordsworth

In my mind's eye I seemed to see him pace
About the weary moors continually,
Wandering about alone and silently.
While I these thoughts within myself pursued,
He, having made a pause, the same discourse renewed.

And soon with this he other matter blended,
Cheerfully uttered, with demeanour kind,
But stately in the main; and, when he ended,
I could have laughed myself to scorn, to find
In that decrepit Man so firm a mind.
"God," said I, "be my help and stay secure;
I'll think of the Leech-gatherer on the lonely moor!"

My heart leaps up when I behold

My heart leaps up when I behold
A rainbow in the sky:
So was it when my life began;
So is it now I am a man;
So be it when I shall grow old,
Or let me die!
The Child is father of the Man;
And I could wish my days to be
Bound each to each by natural piety.

William Wordsworth

It was an April morning: fresh and clear

It was an April morning: fresh and clear
The Rivulet, delighting in its strength,
Ran with a young man's speed; and yet the voice
Of waters which the winter had supplied
Was softened down into a vernal tone.
The spirit of enjoyment and desire,
And hopes and wishes, from all living things
Went circling, like a multitude of sounds.
The budding groves seemed eager to urge on
The steps of June; as if their various hues
Were only hindrances that stood between
Them and their object: but, meanwhile, prevailed
Such an entire contentment in the air
That every naked ash, and tardy tree
Yet leafless, showed as if the countenance
With which it looked on this delightful day
Were native to the summer.—Up the brook
I roamed in the confusion of my heart,
Alive to all things and forgetting all.
At length I to a sudden turning came
In this continuous glen, where down a rock
The Stream, so ardent in its course before,
Sent forth such sallies of glad sound, that all
Which I till then had heard, appeared the voice
Of common pleasure: beast and bird, the lamb,
The shepherd's dog, the linnet and the thrush
Vied with this waterfall, and made a song,
Which, while I listened, seemed like the wild growth
Or like some natural produce of the air,
That could not cease to be. Green leaves were here;

William Wordsworth

But 'twas the foliage of the rocks—the birch,
The yew, the holly, and the bright green thorn,
With hanging islands of resplendent furze:
And, on a summit, distant a short space,
By any who should look beyond the dell,
A single mountain-cottage might be seen.
I gazed and gazed, and to myself I said,
"Our thoughts at least are ours; and this wild nook,
My Emma, I will dedicate to thee."
—Soon did the spot become my other home,
My dwelling, and my out-of-doors abode.
And, of the Shepherds who have seen me there,
To whom I sometimes in our idle talk
Have told this fancy, two or three, perhaps,
Years after we are gone and in our graves,
When they have cause to speak of this wild place,
May call it by the name of Emma's Dell.

William Wordsworth

I wandered lonely as a Cloud

I wandered lonely as a Cloud
That floats on high o'er Vales and Hills,
When all at once I saw a crowd
A host of dancing Daffodills;
Along the Lake, beneath the trees,
Ten thousand dancing in the breeze.

The waves beside them danced, but they
Outdid the sparkling waves in glee:—
A Poet could not but be gay
In such a laughing company:
I gaz'd—and gaz'd—but little thought
What wealth the shew to me had brought:

For oft when on my couch I lie
In vacant or in pensive mood,
They flash upon that inward eye
Which is the bliss of solitude,
And then my heart with pleasure fills,
And dances with the Daffodils.

William Wordsworth

Surprised by Joy

Surprised by joy—impatient as the Wind
I turned to share the transport—Oh! with whom
But Thee, long buried in the silent Tomb,
That spot which no vicissitude can find?
Love, faithful love, recalled thee to my mind—
But how could I forget thee?—Through what power,
Even for the least division of an hour,
Have I been so beguiled as to be blind
To my most grievous loss!—That thought's return
Was the worst pang that sorrow ever bore,
Save one, one only, when I stood forlorn,
Knowing my heart's best treasure was no more;
That neither present time, nor years unborn
Could to my sight that heavenly face restore.

William Wordsworth

Sonnets from The River Duddon: After-Thought

I thought of Thee, my partner and my guide,
As being past away.—Vain sympathies!
For, backward, Duddon! as I cast my eyes,
I see what was, and is, and will abide;
Still glides the Stream, and shall for ever glide;
The Form remains, the Function never dies;
While we, the brave, the mighty, and the wise,
We Men, who in our morn of youth defied
The elements, must vanish;—be it so!
Enough, if something from our hands have power
To live, and act, and serve the future hour;
And if, as toward the silent tomb we go,
Through love, through hope, and faith's
    transcendent dower,
We feel that we are greater than we know.

Robert Anderson
(1770-1833)

The Cummerlan Farmer

TUNE "The lads o' Dunse."

I've thowt an I've thowt, ay, agean an agean,
Sin I was peet-heet, now I see it's queyte plain,
We farmers er happier by far, tho' we're peer,
Than thur they caw gentlefwok, wid aw their gear;
Then, why about riches, aye meake sec a fuss?
Gie us meat, drink, an cleedin; it's plenty fer us—
Frae prince to the plewman, ilk hes but his day;
An when Deeth gie's a beckon, we aw mun obey!

Our darrick's hawf-duin, ere the gentlefwok rise;
We see monie a lark dartin up to the skies;
An blithe as the burd sud aw honest fwok be—
Girt men hae their troubles, as offen as we!
Our weyves an our dowters, we wish to leeve weel;
They tnit, darn, an kurn, or they turn rock an reel:
Our sons niver grummel to toil by our seyde—
May happiness aye the industrious beteyde;

Our youngest lad, Dick, I yence tuik to the town,
He keek'd at shop-windows, an sauntert aw roun,
"Aa, Fadder," says he, "sec a bussle an noise
May flay sair eneugh, aw us peer country bwoys!"
But seebem year aul, yet he daily wad work;
He'll sing owre to schuil, or he'll run to the kurk;
He lissens the parson, an brings heame the text,
I han him the beyble, but Dick's niver vext.

Robert Anderson

In storms, the peer beggars creep up to the fire,
To help sec as thur sud be ilk yen's desire;
They'll smuik a bit peype, an compleen ov hard teymes,
Or tell teales of deevils that glory in creymes;
Expwos'd till aw weathers, they wheyles laugh an jwoke,
Breed, tateys, or wot-meal, we put in the pwoke;
Tho' some are impostors, an daily to bleame,
Frae princes to starvelins, we oft fin the seame.

Our 'squire wid his thousans, keeps jauntin about,
What, he'd give aw his gear, to get shot o' the gout—
Nowther heart-ache nor gout, e'er wi' rakin hed I,
For labour brings that aw his gowd cannot buy!
Then, he'll say to me, "Jacep, thou whissels an sings,
Believe me, you've ten teymes mair plishure nor kings;
I mean honest simplicity, freedom, an health;
Far dearer to man, than the trappings o' wealth!"

Can owt be mair sweet, than leyke larks in a mworn,
To rise wi' the sunsheyne, an luik at the cworn?
Tho' in winter, it's true, dull an lang er the neets,
Yet thro' leyfe, fwok mun aye tek the bitters wi' sweets.
When God grants us plenty, an hous'd are the crops,
How we feast on cruds, collops, an guid buttersops—
Let yer feyne fwok in town brag o' denties whee will,
Content an the country fer mey money still!

They may bwoast o' their gardens as much as they leyke,
Don't flow'rs bloom as fair under onie thworn deyke?
The deil a guid beyte they wad e'er git, I trowe,
Wer't nit fer the peer man that follows the plough,
If we nobbet get plenty, to pay the laird's rent,

Robert Anderson

An keep the bairns teydey, we aye sleep content;
Then ye girt little fwok niver happy in town,
Blush, blush, when ye laugh at a peer country clown!

John Stagg
(1770-1823)

The Wolf and the Shepherd

A wolf, an arrant rogue among the sheep,
  And in the folds a most notorious sinner,
Into a shepherd's cottage chanc'd to peep
One day, as some of them were sate at dinner.

Here were these epicures, in festive glee,
  Regaling on a roasted leg of mutton;
The hungry wolf provok'd to see
A banquet that was so exciting,
Whose look and smell was so inviting,
Was griev'd, as you may think, in his poor gizzard,
And mumbling somewhat like an envious wizard,
  Profoundly curs'd each gormandizing glutton;—
Aye! said the wolf, now would these scurvy scrubs
Have rais'd a pretty clamour at the least,
  Or, what's more like, amid their drubs,
  I should have sunk beneath their clubs,
Had they but found poor me, at such a feast.

Thus, every day, we hear the rogues in power,
  Against the poor plebian rogues exclaim,
Hanging up petty rascals every hour
For various crimes, no matter what,
Sometimes for this, sometimes for that,
  When they, themselves are practicing the same.

Dorothy Wordsworth
(1771-1855)

Floating Island

Harmonious Powers with Nature work
On sky, earth, river, lake, and sea:
Sunshine and storm, whirlwind and breeze
All in one duteous task agree.

Once did I see a slip of earth,
By throbbing waves long undermined,
Loosed from its hold;—how no one knew
But all might see it float, obedient to the wind.

Might see it, from the verdant shore
Dissevered float upon the Lake,
Float, with its crest of trees adorned
On which the warbling birds their pastime take.

Food, shelter, safety there they find
There berries ripen, flowerets bloom;
There insects live their lives—and die:
A peopled world it is;—in size a tiny room.

And thus through many seasons' space
This little Island may survive
But Nature, though we mark her not,
Will take away—may cease to give.

Perchance when you are wandering forth
Upon some vacant sunny day
Without an object, hope, or fear,
Thither your eyes may turn—the Isle is passed away.

Buried beneath the glittering Lake!
Its place no longer to be found,
Yet the lost fragments shall remain,
To fertilize some other ground.

To my Niece Dorothy, a sleepless Baby

The days are cold; the nights are long
The north wind sings a doleful song
Then hush again upon my breast;
All merry things are now at rest
   Save thee my pretty love!

The kitten sleeps upon the hearth;
The crickets long have ceased their mirth
There's nothing stirring in the house
Save one wee hungry nibbling mouse
   Then why so busy thou?

Nay, start not at that sparkling light
'Tis but the moon that shines so bright
On the window-pane bedropp'd with rain
Then, little Darling, sleep again
   And wake when it is Day.

Dorothy Wordsworth

Loving and Liking:
 Irregular Verses Addressed to a Child

There's more in words than I can teach:
But listen Child!—I would not preach;
Yet would I give some plain directions,
To guide your speech and your affections.
Say not you love a roasted fowl,
But you may love a screaming owl,
And, if you can, the unwieldy toad
That crawls from his secure abode
Within the mossy garden wall
When evening dews begin to fall.
Oh! mark the beauty of his eye:
What wonders in that circle lie!
So clear, so bright, our fathers said
He wears a jewel in his head!
And when, upon some showery day,
Into a path or public way
A frog leaps out from bordering grass,
Startling the timid as they pass,
Do you observe him, and endeavour
To take the intruder into favour:
Learning from him to find a reason
For a light heart in a dull season.
And you may love him in the pool,
That is for him a happy school,
In which he swims as taught by nature,
Fit pattern for a human creature,
Glancing amid the water bright,
And sending upward sparkling light.

Dorothy Wordsworth

   Nor blush if o'er your heart be stealing
A love for things that have no feeling:
The spring's first rose by you espied,
May fill your breast with joyful pride;
And you may love the strawberry-flower,
And love the strawberry in its bower;
But when the fruit, so often praised
For beauty, to your lip is raised,
Say not you love the delicate treat,
But like it, enjoy it, and thankfully eat.

   Long may you love your pensioner mouse,
Though one of a tribe that torment the house:
Nor dislike for her cruel sport the cat
Deadly foe both of mouse and rat;
Remember she follows the law of her kind,
And Instinct is neither wayward nor blind.
Then think of her beautiful gliding form,
Her tread that would scarcely crush a worm,
And her soothing song by the winter fire,
Soft as the dying throb of the lyre.

   I would not circumscribe your love:
It may soar with the Eagle and brood with the dove,
May pierce the earth with the patient mole,
Or track the hedgehog to his hole.
Loving and liking are the solace of life,
Rock the cradle of joy, smooth the death-bed of strife.
You love your father and your mother,
Your grown-up and your baby brother;
You love your sister and your friends,
And countless blessings which God sends;

And while these right affections play,
You live each moment of your day;
They lead you on to full content,
And likings fresh and innocent,
That store the mind, the memory feed,
And prompt to many a gentle deed:
But likings come, and pass away;
'Tis love that remains till our latest day:
Our heavenward guide is holy love,
And will be our bliss with saints above.

Dorothy Wordsworth

Thoughts on my Sick-bed

And has the remnant of my life
Been pilfered of this sunny Spring?
And have its own prelusive sounds
Touched in my heart no echoing string?

Ah! say not so—the hidden life
Couchant within this feeble frame
Hath been enriched by kindred gifts,
That, undesired, unsought-for, came

With joyful heart in youthful days
When fresh each season in its Round
I welcomed the earliest Celandine
Glittering upon the mossy ground;

With busy eyes I pierced the lane
In quest of known and unknown things,
—The primrose a lamp on its fortress rock,
The silent butterfly spreading its wings,

The violet betrayed by its noiseless breath,
The daffodil dancing in the breeze,
The carolling thrush, on his naked perch,
Towering above the budding trees.

Our cottage-hearth no longer our home,
Companions of Nature were we,
The Stirring, the Still, the Loquacious, the Mute—
To all we gave our sympathy.

Yet never in those careless days
When spring-time in rock, field, or bower
Was but a fountain of earthly hope
A promise of fruits & the splendid flower.

Dorothy Wordsworth

No! then I never felt a bliss
That might with that compare
Which, piercing to my couch of rest,
Came on the vernal air.

When loving Friends an offering brought,
The first flowers of the year,
Culled from the precincts of our home,
From nooks to Memory dear.

With some sad thoughts the work was done.
Unprompted and unbidden,
But joy it brought to my hidden life,
To consciousness no longer hidden.

I felt a power unfelt before,
Controlling weakness, languor, pain;
It bore me to the Terrace walk
I trod the hills again;—

No prisoner in this lonely room,
I saw the green Banks of the Wye,
Recalling thy prophetic words,
Bard, Brother, Friend from infancy!

No need of motion, or of strength,
Or even the breathing air;
—I thought of Nature's loveliest scenes;
And with Memory I was there.

Dorothy Wordsworth

When shall I tread your garden path...

When shall I tread your garden path?
Or climb your sheltering hill?
When shall I wander, free as air,
And track the foaming rill?

A prisoner on my pillowed couch
Five years in feebleness I've lain,
Oh! shall I e'er with vigorous step
Travel the hills again?

Samuel Taylor Coleridge
(1772-1834)

Dejection: An Ode

> Late, late yestreen I saw the new Moon,
> With the old Moon in her arms;
> And I fear, I fear, my Master dear!
> We shall have a deadly storm.
> *Ballad of Sir Patrick Spence*

I
Well! If the Bard was weather-wise, who made
    The grand old ballad of Sir Patrick Spence,
    This night, so tranquil now, will not go hence
Unroused by winds, that ply a busier trade
Than those which mould yon cloud in lazy flakes,
Or the dull sobbing draft, that moans and rakes
Upon the strings of this Æolian lute,
        Which better far were mute.
    For lo! the New-moon winter-bright!
    And overspread with phantom light,
    (With swimming phantom light o'erspread
    But rimmed and circled by a silver thread)
I see the old Moon in her lap, foretelling
    The coming-on of rain and squally blast.
And oh! that even now the gust were swelling,
    And the slant night-shower driving loud and fast!
Those sounds which oft have raised me, whilst they awed,
    And sent my soul abroad,
Might now perhaps their wonted impulse give,
Might startle this dull pain, and make it move and live!

II

A grief without a pang, void, dark, and drear,
    A stifled, drowsy, unimpassioned grief,
      Which finds no natural outlet, no relief,
        In word, or sigh, or tear—
O Lady! in this wan and heartless mood,
To other thoughts by yonder throstle wooed,
    All this long eve, so balmy and serene,
Have I been gazing on the western sky,
    And its peculiar tint of yellow green:
And still I gaze—and with how blank an eye!
And those thin clouds above, in flakes and bars,
That give away their motion to the stars;
Those stars, that glide behind them or between,
Now sparkling, now bedimmed, but always seen:
Yon crescent Moon, as fixed as if it grew
In its own cloudless, starless lake of blue;
I see them all so excellently fair,
I see, not feel, how beautiful they are!

III

    My genial spirits fail;
    And what can these avail
To lift the smothering weight from off my breast?
    It were a vain endeavour,
    Though I should gaze for ever
On that green light that lingers in the west:
I may not hope from outward forms to win
The passion and the life, whose fountains are within.

Samuel Taylor Coleridge

IV

O Lady! we receive but what we give,
And in our life alone does Nature live:
Ours is her wedding garment, ours her shroud!
    And would we aught behold, of higher worth,
Than that inanimate cold world allowed
To the poor loveless ever-anxious crowd,
    Ah! from the soul itself must issue forth
A light, a glory, a fair luminous cloud
        Enveloping the Earth—
And from the soul itself must there be sent
    A sweet and potent voice, of its own birth,
Of all sweet sounds the life and element!

V

O pure of heart! thou need'st not ask of me
What this strong music in the soul may be!
What, and wherein it doth exist,
This light, this glory, this fair luminous mist,
This beautiful and beauty-making power.
    Joy, virtuous Lady! Joy that ne'er was given,
Save to the pure, and in their purest hour,
Life, and Life's effluence, cloud at once and shower,
Joy, Lady! is the spirit and the power,
Which wedding Nature to us gives in dower
    A new Earth and new Heaven,
Undreamt of by the sensual and the proud—
Joy is the sweet voice, Joy the luminous cloud—
        We in ourselves rejoice!
And thence flows all that charms or ear or sight,
    All melodies the echoes of that voice,
All colours a suffusion from that light.

VI

There was a time when, though my path was rough,
    This joy within me dallied with distress,
And all misfortunes were but as the stuff
    Whence Fancy made me dreams of happiness:
For hope grew round me, like the twining vine,
And fruits, and foliage, not my own, seemed mine.
But now afflictions bow me down to earth:
Nor care I that they rob me of my mirth;
    But oh! each visitation
Suspends what nature gave me at my birth,
    My shaping spirit of Imagination.
For not to think of what I needs must feel,
    But to be still and patient, all I can;
And haply by abstruse research to steal
    From my own nature all the natural man—
    This was my sole resource, my only plan:
Till that which suits a part infects the whole,
And now is almost grown the habit of my soul.

VII

Hence, viper thoughts, that coil around my mind,
    Reality's dark dream!
I turn from you, and listen to the wind,
    Which long has raved unnoticed. What a scream
Of agony by torture lengthened out
That lute sent forth! Thou Wind, that rav'st without,
    Bare crag, or mountain-tairn, or blasted tree,
Or pine-grove whither woodman never clomb,
Or lonely house, long held the witches' home,
    Methinks were fitter instruments for thee,
Mad Lutanist! who in this month of showers,

Samuel Taylor Coleridge

Of dark-brown gardens, and of peeping flowers,
Mak'st Devils' yule, with worse than wintry song,
The blossoms, buds, and timorous leaves among.
    Thou Actor, perfect in all tragic sounds!
Thou mighty Poet, e'en to frenzy bold!
        What tell'st thou now about?
        'Tis of the rushing of an host in rout,
With groans, of trampled men, with smarting wounds—
At once they groan with pain, and shudder with the cold!
But hush! there is a pause of deepest silence!
    And all that noise, as of a rushing crowd,
With groans, and tremulous shudderings—all is over—
      It tells another tale, with sounds less deep and loud!
      A tale of less affright,
      And tempered with delight,
As Otway's self had framed the tender lay,—
      'Tis of a little child
      Upon a lonesome wild,
Nor far from home, but she hath lost her way:
And now moans low in bitter grief and fear,
And now screams loud, and hopes to make her mother hear.

VIII

'Tis midnight, but small thoughts have I of sleep:
Full seldom may my friend such vigils keep!
Visit her, gentle Sleep! with wings of healing,
    And may this storm be but a mountain-birth,
May all the stars hang bright above her dwelling,
    Silent as though they watched the sleeping Earth!
      With light heart may she rise,
      Gay fancy, cheerful eyes,

> Joy lift her spirit, joy attune her voice;
> To her may all things live, from pole to pole,
> Their life the eddying of her living soul!
> O simple spirit, guided from above,
> Dear Lady! friend devoutest of my choice,
> Thus mayest thou ever, evermore rejoice.

Samuel Taylor Coleridge

To Asra

Are there two things, of all which men possess,
That are so like each other and so near,
As mutual Love seems like to Happiness?
Dear Asra, woman beyond utterance dear!
This love which ever welling at my heart,
Now in its living fount doth heave and fall,
Now overflowing pours thro' every part
Of all my frame, and fills and changes all,
Like vernal waters springing up through snow,
This Love that seeming great beyond the power
Of growth, yet seemeth ever more to grow,
Could I transmute the whole to one rich Dower
Of Happy Life, and give it all to Thee,
Thy lot, methinks, were Heaven, thy age, Eternity!

Samuel Taylor Coleridge

A Sunset

Upon the mountain's Edge all lightly resting
There a brief while the Globe of splendour sits,
And seems a creature of this earth; but soon
More changeful than the Moon
To Wane fantastic his great orb submits,
Or cone or mow of Fire, till sinking slowly
Even to a Star at length he lessens wholly.

Abrupt, as Spirits vanish, he is sunk
A soul-like breeze possesses all the wood;
The Boughs, the sprays have stood
As motionless, as stands the ancient Trunk,
But every leaf thro' all the forest flutters,
And deep the Cavern of the Fountain mutters.

Samuel Taylor Coleridge

A Thought Suggested by a View of Saddleback in Cumberland

On stern Blencathra's perilous height
The winds are tyrannous and strong;
And flashing forth unsteady light
From stern Blencathra's skiey height,
As loud the torrents throng!
Beneath the moon, in gentle weather,
They bind the earth and sky together.
But oh! the sky and all is forms, how quiet!
The things that seek the earth, how full of noise and riot!

Samuel Taylor Coleridge

Frost at Midnight

The frost performs its secret ministry,
Unhelped by any wind. The owlet's cry
Came loud—and hark, again! loud as before.
The inmates of my cottage, all at rest,
Have left me to that solitude, which suits
Abstruser musings: save that at my side
My cradled infant slumbers peacefully.
'Tis calm indeed! so calm, that it disturbs
And vexes meditation with its strange
And extreme silentness. Sea, hill, and wood,
This populous village! Sea, and hill, and wood,
With all the numberless goings-on of life,
Inaudible as dreams! the thin blue flame
Lies on my low-burnt fire, and quivers not;
Only that film, which fluttered on the grate,
Still flutters there, the sole unquiet thing.
Methinks, its motion in this hush of nature
Gives it dim sympathies with me who live,
Making it a companionable form,
Whose puny flaps and freaks the idling Spirit
By its own moods interprets, everywhere
Echo or mirror seeking of itself,
And makes a toy of Thought.

                      But O! how oft,
How oft, at school, with most believing mind,
Presageful, have I gazed upon the bars,
To watch that fluttering stranger! and as oft
With unclosed lids, already had I dreamt
Of my sweet birthplace, and the old church-tower,

Samuel Taylor Coleridge

Whose bells, the poor man's only music, rang
From morn to evening, all the hot Fair-day,
So sweetly, that they stirred and haunted me
With a wild pleasure, falling on mine ear
Most like articulate sounds of things to come!
So gazed I, till the soothing things I dreamt
Lulled me to sleep, and sleep prolonged my dreams!
And so I brooded all the following morn,
Awed by the stern preceptor's face, mine eye
Fixed with mock study on my swimming book:
Save if the door half opened, and I snatched
A hasty glance, and still my heart leaped up,
For still I hoped to see the stranger's face,
Townsman, or aunt, or sister more beloved,
My playmate when we both were clothed alike!

  Dear babe, that sleepest cradled by my side,
Whose gentle breathings, heard in this deep calm,
Fill up the interspersed vacancies
And momentary pauses of the thought!
My babe so beautiful! it thrills my heart
With tender gladness, thus to look at thee,
And think that thou shalt learn far other lore
And in far other scenes! For I was reared
In the great city, pent 'mid cloisters dim,
And saw nought lovely but the sky and stars.
But thou, my babe! shalt wander like a breeze
By lakes and sandy shores, beneath the crags
Of ancient mountain, and beneath the clouds,
Which image in their bulk both lakes and shores
And mountain crags: so shalt thou see and hear
The lovely shapes and sounds intelligible

Samuel Taylor Coleridge

Of that eternal language, which thy God
Utters, who fro eternity doth teach
Himself in all, and all things in himself.
Great universal Teacher! he shall mould
They spirit, and by giving make it ask.

   Therefore all seasons shall be sweet to thee,
Whether the summer clothe the general earth
With greenness, or the redbreast sit and sing
Betwixt the tufts of snow on the bare branch
Of mossy apple-tree, while the nigh thatch
Smokes in the sunthaw; whether the eve-drops fall
Heard only in the trances of the blast,
Or if the secret ministry of frost
Shall hang them up in silent icicles,
Quietly shining to the quiet Moon.

Robert Southey
(1774-1843)

from The Poet's Pilgrimage to Waterloo: Proem

Once more I see thee, Skiddaw! once again
Behold thee in thy majesty serene,
Where like the bulwark of this favoured plain,
Alone thou standest, monarch of the scene,—
Thou glorious Mountain, on whose ample breast
The sunbeams love to play, the vapours love to rest!

Once more, O Derwent! to thy aweful shores
I come, insatiate of the accustomed sight;
And listening as the eternal torrent roars,
Drink in with eye and ear a fresh delight:
For I have wandered far by land and sea,
In all my wanderings still remembering thee.

Twelve years, (how large a part of man's brief day!)
Nor idly, nor ingloriously spent,
Of evil and of good have held their way,
Since first upon thy banks I pitched my tent.
Hither I came in manhood's active prime,
And here my head hath felt the touch of time.

Heaven hath with goodly increase blest me here,
Where childless and opprest with grief I came;
With voice of fervent thankfulness sincere
Let me the blessings which are mine proclaim:
Here I possess—what more should I require?—
Books, children, leisure,—all my heart's desire.

Robert Southey

O joyful hour, when to our longing home
The long-expected wheels at length drew nigh!
When the first sound went forth, "They come, they come!"
And hope's impatience quickened every eye!
"Never had man whom Heaven would heap with bliss
More glad return, more happy hour than this."

Robert Southey

Epitaph

HERE, in the fruitful vales of Somerset,
Was Emma born, and here the maiden grew
To the sweet season of her womanhood,
Beloved and lovely, like a plant whose leaf
And bud and blossom all are beautiful.
In peacefulness her virgin years were passed;
And, when in prosperous wedlock she was given,
Amid the Cumbrian mountains far away
She had her summer bower. 'Twas like a dream
Of old romance to see her when she plied
Her little skiff on Derwent's glassy lake;
The roseate evening resting on the hills,
The lake returning back the hues of heaven,
Mountains and vales and waters, all imbued
With beauty, and in quietness; and she,
Nymph-like, amid that glorious solitude
A heavenly presence, gliding in her joy.
But soon a wasting malady began
To prey upon her, frequent in attack,
Yet with such flattering intervals as mock
The hopes of anxious love, and most of all
The sufferer, self-deceived. During those days
Of treacherous respite, many a time hath he,
Who leaves this record of his friend, drawn back
Into the shadow from her social board,
Because too surely in her cheek he saw
The insidious bloom of death; and then her smiles
And innocent mirth excited deeper grief
Than when long-looked-for tidings came at last,
That, all her sufferings ended, she was laid

Amid Madeira's orange-groves to rest.
O gentle Emma! o'er a lovelier form
Than thine earth never closed; nor e'er did heaven
Receive a purer spirit from the world.

Spring

Thou lingerest, Spring! still wintry is the scene,
The fields their dead and sapless russet wear;
Scarce does the glossy Celandine appear
Starring the sunny bank, or, early green
The elder yet its circling tufts put forth,
The sparrow tenants still the eave-built nest
Where we should see our martin's snowy breast
Oft darting out. The blasts from the bleak North
And from the keener East still frequent blow.
Sweet Spring, thou lingerest; and it should be so—
Late let the fields and gardens blossom out!
Like man when most with smiles thy face is drest,
'Tis to deceive, and he who knows ye best.
When most ye promise, ever most must doubt.

Robert Southey

My days among the Dead are Past

My days among the Dead are past;
　　Around me I behold,
Where'er these casual eyes are cast,
　　The mighty minds of old;
My never-failing friends are they,
With whom I converse day by day.

With them I take delight in weal,
　　And seek relief in woe;
And while I understand and feel
　　How much to them I owe,
My cheeks have often been bedew'd
With tears of thoughtful gratitude.

My thoughts are with the Dead, with them
　　I live in long-past years,
Their virtues love, their faults condemn,
　　Partake their hopes and fears,
And from their lessons seek and find
Instruction with an humble mind.

My hopes are with the Dead, anon
　　My place with them will be,
And I with them shall travel on
　　Through all Futurity;
Yet leaving here a name, I trust,
That will not perish in the dust.

Robert Southey

The Cataract of Lodore

"How does the water
 Come down at Lodore?"
My little boy asked me
Thus, once on a time;
And moreover he tasked me
To tell him in rhyme.
Anon, at the word,
There first came one daughter,
And then came another,
To second and third
The request of their brother,
And to hear how the water
Comes down at Lodore,
With its rush and its roar,
As many a time
They had seen it before.
So I told them in rhyme,
For of rhymes I had store;
And 'twas in my vocation
For their recreation
That so I should sing;
Because I was Laureate
To them and the King.

From its sources which well
In the tarn on the fell;
From its fountains
In the mountains,
Its rills and its gills;
Through moss and through brake,
It runs and it creeps

Robert Southey

For a while, till it sleeps
In its own little lake.
And thence at departing,
Awakening and starting,
It runs through the reeds,
And away it proceeds,
Through meadow and glade,
In sun and in shade,
And through the wood-shelter,
Among crags in its flurry,
Helter-skelter,
Hurry-skurry.
Here it comes sparkling,
And there it lies darkling;
Now smoking and frothing
Its tumult and wrath in,
Till, in this rapid race
On which it is bent,
It reaches the place
Of its steep descent.

The cataract strong
Then plunges along,
Striking and raging

As if a war raging
Its caverns and rocks among;
Rising and leaping,
Sinking and creeping,
Swelling and sweeping,
Showering and springing,
Flying and flinging,
Writhing and ringing,
Eddying and whisking,

Spouting and frisking,
Turning and twisting,
Around and around
With endless rebound:
Smiting and fighting,
A sight to delight in;
Confounding, astounding,
Dizzying and deafening the ear with its sound.

Collecting, projecting,
Receding and speeding,
And shocking and rocking,
And darting and parting,
And threading and spreading,
And whizzing and hissing,
And dripping and skipping,
And hitting and splitting,
And shining and twining,
And rattling and battling,
And shaking and quaking,
And pouring and roaring,
And waving and raving,
And tossing and crossing,
And flowing and going,
And running and stunning,
And foaming and roaming,
And dinning and spinning,
And dropping and hopping,
And working and jerking,
And guggling and struggling,
And heaving and cleaving,
And moaning and groaning;

Robert Southey

And glittering and frittering,
And gathering and feathering,
And whitening and brightening,
And quivering and shivering,
And hurrying and skurrying,
And thundering and floundering;

Dividing and gliding and sliding,
And falling and brawling and sprawling,
And driving and riving and striving,
And sprinkling and twinkling and wrinkling,
And sounding and bounding and rounding,
And bubbling and troubling and doubling,
And grumbling and rumbling and tumbling,
And clattering and battering and shattering;

Retreating and beating and meeting and sheeting,
Delaying and straying and playing and spraying,
Advancing and prancing and glancing and dancing,
Recoiling, turmoiling and toiling and boiling,
And gleaming and streaming and steaming and beaming,
And rushing and flushing and brushing and gushing,
And flapping and rapping and clapping and slapping,
And curling and whirling and purling and twirling,
And thumping and plumping and bumping and jumping,
And dashing and flashing and splashing and clashing;
And so never ending, but always descending,
Sounds and motions for ever and ever are blending
All at once and all o'er, with a mighty uproar, -
And this way the water comes down at Lodore.

Isabella Lickbarrow
(1784-1847)

On Esthwaite Water

O'er Esthwaite's lake, serene and still,
At sunset's silent peaceful hour,
Scarce moved the zephyr's softest breath,
Or sighed along its reedy shore.

The lovely landscape on its sides,
With evening's softening hues impressed,
Shared in the general calm, and gave
Sweet visions of repose and rest.

Inverted on the waveless flood,
A spotless mirror smooth and clear,
Each fair surrounding object shone
In softer beauty imaged there.

Brown hills and woods of various shades,
Orchards and sloping meadows green,
Sweet rural seats, and sheltered farms,
Were in the bright reflector seen.

E'en lofty Tilberthwaite from far
His giant shadow boldly threw,
His rugged, dark, high-towering head
On Esthwaite's tranquil breast to view.

Isabella Lickbarrow

Struck with the beauty of the scene,
I cried, Oh! may my yielding breast
Retain but images of peace
Like those, sweet lake, on thine impressed!

Ne'er may it feel a ruder gale
Than that which o'er thy surface spreads,
When sportive zephyrs briskly play,
And whisper through thy bordering reeds;

When, dancing in the solar beam,
Thy silvery waves the margin seek,
With gently undulating flow,
And there in softest murmurs break.

Vain wish! o'er Esthwaite's tranquil lake,
A stronger gale full frequent blows,
The soothing prospect disappears,
The lovely visions of repose!

Written In A Cemetery

In this lone unfrequented spot
Amongst these dwellings of the dead,
Does spring her beauteous charms display,
And here her fragrant odours shed.

She hangs the blossoms on the trees
Which o'er the mould'ring ashes wave;
She paints the leaves with vivid green,
And strews with flowers the lowly grave.

But ah! to those who slumber here,
The simple flowers which deck the plain,
The verdant foliage of the trees,
And golden blossoms, blow in vain.

And ye gay tenants of the grove,
Sweet minstrels of the early year,
In vain ye pour the tuneful strain,
For they, alas! can never hear.

Ye dwellers in these lowly cells,
When wintry tempests round you sweep,
In death's oblivious slumbers wrapp'd,
Ah! how securely then you sleep

Tho' long and loud the thunder rolls
Around the dark and troubled sky,
And bursting from the fiery cloud,
The forked light'ning flashes by;

Should whirlwinds rend the rooted trees,
And earthquakes rock the trembling ground,
The noise of elemental strife,
Can never break your rest profound.

Isabella Lickbarrow

Tho' war's dread tempest loudly roars,
And rages round th' affrighted world;
Tho' nations tremble at the sound,
And monarchs from their thrones be hurl'd,

You know it not—for quiet peace
Within the grave for ever reigns;
No hostile sounds can e'er invade
The silence of death's still domains.

The anxious never ceasing cares,
Invaders of the human breast;
Doubt, and solicitude, and fear,
Here slumber in perpetual rest.

No more shall anguish rend the heart,
Or sink the spirit in despair,
No more the mind shall droop beneath
Stern disappointment's frown severe.

O'er scenes of complicated woe,
No more the feeling heart shall grieve,
Nor breathe the unavailing sigh,
For mis'ries which it can't relieve.

Mourn not, ye living, for the dead,
Their day of toil and trouble o'er,
Sweet are their slumbers in the grave,
And they awake to grief no more.

John Wilson (Christopher North)
(1785-1854)

Wastwater in a Storm

There is a lake hid far among the hills,
That raves around the throne of solitude,
Not fed by gentle streams, or playful rills,
But headlong cataract and rushing flood:
There gleam no lovely hues of hanging wood,
No spot of sunshine lights her sullen side
For horror shaped the wild in wrathful mood,
And o'er the tempest heaved the mountain's pride.
If thou art one, in dark presumption blind,
Who vainly deem'st no spirit like to thine,
That lofty genius deifies thy mind,
Fall prostrate here at Nature's stormy shrine,
And, as the thunderous scene disturbs thy heart,
Lift thy changed eye, and own how low thou art.

John Wilson

Wastwater in a Calm

Is this the lake, the cradle of the storms,
Where silence never tames the mountain-roar,
Where poets fear their self-created forms,
Or, sunk in trance severe, their God adore?
Is this the lake, for ever dark and loud
With wave and tempest, cataract and cloud?
Wondrous, O Nature! is thy sovereign power,
That gives to horror hours of peaceful mirth;
For here might beauty build her summer-bower!
Lo! where yon rainbow spans the smiling earth,
And, clothed in glory, through a silent shower
The mighty Sun comes forth, a godlike birth;
While, 'neath his loving eye, the gentle Lake
Lies like a sleeping child too blest to wake!

Edward Quillinan
(1791-1851)

The Birch of Silver How

I'll doubt no more that Fairies dwell
At least in one enchanted place,
Though wisdom long since rang the knell
Of Oberon and all his race:
They haunt Kehlbarrow's woody brow,
Amid the rocks of Silver-How!

And if you climb beyond the wood
You'll there a Fairy chapel see;
And there, in spite of wind and flood,
Beside it find a goodly tree:
Of upright stem and flexile bough,
The Fairy-tree of Silver-How.

A night of tempest shook the hills
That circle Grasmere's lovely lake;
To torrents swoln, the flashing rills
Went chafing down o'er stone and brake:
When morning peep'd o'er Fairfield's brow
Low lay the birch of Silver-How!

The red-breast that was wont to sing
His matins on its topmost spray,
Now wheel'd aloof his fickle wing
To chaunt elsewhere his roundelay:
To thriving trees his court he paid
So well he knew the poet's trade. The Sun went

Edward Quillinan

down, but when again
He rose and look'd on Silver-How,
The red-breast trill'd his morning strain
Upon his old accustom'd bough:
For lo! the tree that prostrate lay,
Erectly stood in face of day.

It rose, untouch'd by human hands.
And now a living wonder stands
On that enchanted Fell!

Wise sceptic, you deny in vain
To wild Kehlbarrow's fairy fane
A priestess and a spell:
Go profit by my elfin creed,
And lift the fallen in their need
As secretly and well!

Felicia Hemans
(1793-1835)

A Remembrance of Grasmere

O vale and lake, within your mountain-urn
Smiling so tranquilly, and set so deep!
Oft doth your dreamy loveliness return,
Colouring the tender shadows of my sleep
With light Elysian:—for the hues that steep
Your shores in melting lustre seem to float
On golden clouds from Spirit-lands remote,
Isles of the blest;—and in our memory keep
Their place with holiest harmonies:—Fair scene,
Most lov'd by evening and her dewy star!
Oh! ne'er may man, with touch unhallow'd, jar
The perfect music of the charm serene!
Still, still unchanged, may one sweet region wear
Smiles that subdue the soul to love, and tears, and prayer!

Felicia Hemans

To Wordsworth

There is a strain to read among the hills,
The old and full of voices—by the source
Of some free stream, whose gladdening presence fills
The solitude with sound; for in its course
Even such is thy deep song, that seems a part
Of those high scenes, a fountain from the heart.

Or its calm spirit fitly may be taken
To the still breast in sunny garden bowers,
Where vernal winds each tree's low tones awaken,
And bud and bell with changes mark the hours.
There let thy thoughts be with me, while the day
Sinks with a golden and serene decay.

Or by some hearth where happy faces meet,
When night hath hushed the woods, with all their birds,
There, from some gentle voice, that lay were sweet
As antique music, linked with household words;
While in pleased murmurs woman's lip might move,
And the raised eye of childhood shine in love.

Or where the shadows of dark solemn yews
Brood silently o'er some lone burial-ground,
Thy verse hath power that brightly might diffuse
A breath, a kindling, as of spring, around;
From its own glow of hope and courage high,
And steadfast faith's victorious constancy.

Felicia Hemans

True bard and holy!—thou art e'en as one
Who, by some secret gift of soul or eye,
In every spot beneath the smiling sun,
Sees where the springs of living waters lie;
Unseen awhile they sleep—till, touched by thee,
Bright healthful waves flow forth, to each glad
      wanderer free.

Hartley Coleridge
(1796-1849)

Dedicatory Sonnet to S.T. Coleridge

Father, and Bard revered! to whom I owe,
Whate'er it may be, my little art of numbers.
Thou, in thy night-watch o'er my cradled slumbers,
Didst meditate the verse that lives to show
(And long shall live, when we alike are low)
Thy prayer how ardent, and thy hopes how strong.
That I should learn of Nature's self the song,
The love which none but Nature's pupils know.
The prayer was heard: I 'wandered like a breeze'
By mountain brooks and solitary meres.
And gathered there the shapes and fantasies
Which, mixed with passions of my sadder years,
Compose this book. If good therein there be,
That good, my sire, I dedicate to thee.

Hartley Coleridge

Long time a child, and still a child, when years

Long time a child, and still a child, when years
Had painted manhood on my cheek, was I,—
For yet I lived like one not born to die;
A thriftless prodigal of smiles and tears,
No hope I needed, and I knew no fears.
But sleep, though sweet, is only sleep, and waking,
I waked to sleep no more, at once o'ertaking
The vanguard of my age, with all arrears
Of duty on my back. Nor child, nor man,
Nor youth, nor sage, I find my head is grey,
For I have lost the race I never ran:
A rathe December blights my lagging May;
And still I am a child, tho' I be old,
Time is my debtor for my years untold.

Hartley Coleridge

To A Friend Leaving Grasmere

Sweet Grasmere vale, though I must leave
  Thy hills and quiet waters,
Nor sing again at fragrant eve
  To glad thy winsome daughters,
Yet will I fondly think of thee,
And thy fair maids will think of me,
When I am far away.

I think of thee, but 'tis a thought
  That has no touch of sadness;
I joy to think that I have brought
  To thee so much of gladness.
Such thoughts I fain would leave behind
To maidens that are fair and kind,
When I am far away.

Hartley Coleridge

Lines Written Impromptu After Hearing A Lady Singing

Like a blithe birdie in a darksome isle
Of changeless holly mid a spacious wood;
Such was the song, and such the pensive smile,
Robed in the garb of early widowhood.
And yet not so, the birdie has a nest,
And sings of hopes and joys that yet are coming,
When every bush is in its vernal best,
And all her callow brood are sunk to rest
To thousand thousand insects' joyous humming.
But not in hope the human songstress trills
The lilt of joy, or long, long note of sorrow;
We sing not well till frequent proofs of ills
Have made us too distrustful of to-morrow;
And yet sometimes we gladly would be gay–
So let's rejoice in joy of yesterday.

William Dickinson
(1799-1882)

The Words of Oald Cummerlan'

Ya neet I was takkan a rist an' a smeuk,
An' snoozlan an' beekan my shins at t' grate neuk,
When I thowt I wad knock up a bit of a beuk
About t' words 'at we use in oald Cummerlan'.

I boddert my brains thinkan some o' them ower,
An' than set to wark an' wreatt doon three or fower
O' t' kaymtest an' t' creuktest, like "garrak" an' "dyke stower,"
Sek like as we use in oald Cummerlan'.

It turnt oot three corner't, cantankerous wark,
An' keep't yan at thinkin frae dayleet till dark
An' at times a queer word wad lowp up wi' a yark,
'At was reet ebm down like oald Cummerlan'.

John Dixon o' Whitten poot out of his kist,
O' words 'at he thowt to hev prentit, a list:
An' rayder ner any reet word sud be mist,
Yan wad ratch iv'ry neuk of oald Cummerlan'.

Than Deavvy frae Steappleton hitch in a lock,
An' Jwony of Rougham gave some to my stock;
Than frae Castle Graystick a list com—frae Jock;
They o' eekt a share for oald Cummerlan'.

Friend Rannelson offert his beuks, an' o' t' rest,
(O man! bit he's full of oald stwories—ey, t' best,)

William Dickinson

I teuk him at word, an' I harry't his nest
Of oald-farrant words of oald Cummerlan'.

Than naybers an' friends browt words in sa fast,
An' chatter't an' laught till they varra nar brast,
To think what a beuk wad come out on't at last—
Full o' nowt bit oald words o' oald Cummerlan'.

Than, who can e'er read it—can any yan tell?
Nay, niver a body bit t' writer his-sel!
An' what can be t' use if it o' be to spell
Afoor yan can read its oald Cummerlan'?

Workington,
July 15th, 1859

Sara Coleridge
(1802-1852)

The Months

January brings the snow,
Makes our feet and fingers glow.

February brings the rain,
Thaws the frozen lake again.

March brings breezes, loud and shrill,
Stirs the dancing daffodil.

April brings the primrose sweet,
Scatters daisies at our feet.

May brings flocks of pretty lambs,
Skipping by their fleecy dams.

June brings tulips, lilies, roses,
Fills the children's hands with posies.

Hot July brings cooling showers,
Apricots and gilliflowers.

August brings the sheaves of corn,
Then the harvest home is borne.

Warm September brings the fruit,
Sportsmen then begin to shoot.

Sara Coleridge

Fresh October brings the pheasant,
Then to gather nuts is pleasant.

Dull November brings the blast,
Then the leaves are whirling fast.

Chill December brings the sleet,
Blazing fire, and Christmas treat.

Letitia Elizabeth Landon (L.E.L.)
(1802-1838)

Coniston Water

Thou lone and lovely water, would I were
A dweller by thy deepest solitude!
How weary am I of my present life,
Its falsehoods, and its fantasies—its noise,
And the unkindly hurry of the crowd,
'Mid whom my days are numbered! I would watch
The tremulous vibration of the rays
The moon sends down to kiss thy quiet waves;
And when they died, wish I could die like them,
Melting upon the still and silvery air:
Or when the autumn scatters the wan leaves
Like ghosts, I'd meditate above their fall,
And say "So perish all our earthly hopes."
So is the heart left desolate and bare,
And on us falls the shadow of the tomb,
Before we rest within it—

John Richardson
(1817-1886)

"It's Nobbut Me!"

Ya winter neet, I mind it weel,
Oor lads hed been at t' fell,
An', bein' tir't, went seun to bed,
An' I sat be mysel.
I hard a jike on t' window pane,
An' deftly went to see;
An' when I ax't, "Who's jiken theer?"
Says t' chap, "It's nobbut me!"

"Who's me?" says I, "What want ye here?
Oor fwok ur aw I' bed;"—
"I dunnet want your fwok at aw,
It's thee I want," he sed.
"What cant'e want wi'me," says I;
"An' who, the deuce, can't be?
Just tell me who it is, an' than"—
Says he, "Its nobbut me."

"I want a sweetheart, an' I thowt
Thoo mebby wad an' aw;
I'd been a bit down t' deal to-neet,
An' thowt 'at I wad caw;
What, cant'e like me, dus t'e think?
I think I wad like thee"—
"I dunnet know who 't is," says I,
Says he, "It's nobbut me."

John Richardson

We pestit on a canny while,
I thowt his voice I kent;
An' than I steall quite whisht away,
An' oot at t' dooer I went
I creapp, an' gat him be t' cwoat laps,
'Twas dark, he cuddent see;
He startit roond, an' said, "Who's that?"
Says I, "It's nobbut me."

An' menny a time he com ageann,
An' menny a time I went,
An' sed, "Who's that 'at's jiken theer?"
When gaily weel I kent:
An' mainly what t' seamm answer com,
Fra back o' t' laylick tree;
He sed, "I think thoo knows who't is:
Thoo knows it's nobbut me."

It's twenty year an' mair sen than,
An' ups an' doons we've hed;
An' six fine barns hev blest us beatth.
Sen Jim an' me war wed.
An' menny a time I've known him steal.
When I'd yan on me knee.
To mak me start, an' than wad laugh—
Ha! ha! "It's nobbut me."

Edmund Lee
(1844-1931)

To F.H. (By The Wishing Gate)

We lingered by the Wishing Gate,
One happy eve of May,
In that fair spot where memories wait,
And wield a potent sway.

Old-time tradition o'er us flung
The influence of its spell,
As if in truth the future hung
On what our wishes tell.

Dear maiden, standing by my side,
Before the Wishing Gate,
If longing fair could rule thy tide,
Then bright would be thy fate.

But well I know a rarer charm
Than wish of friend most true,
Which will for life's stern battle arm,
And aye thy youth renew.

The love alone of this bright scene,
Touched by enchanter's spell,
Will help to make they heart serene,
Where happy thoughts shall dwell.

And love of truth and purity,
Of fairest things around,

Will make for all futurity
The earth a hallowed ground.

And so the memory of this night,
Of lake, of wood, of mount,
May live to give thy soul delight,
Of gladness be a fount.

Edmund Lee

In Grasmere Churchyard

Once more by Rothay's "living wave,"
Which flows hard by our Wordsworth's grave,
I pause, and think with thankful heart,
Of what in life hath been my part.

Since boyhood's days my feet have trod
The well-worn paths to this green sod;
And so with every passing year
The scenes around become more dear.

The best that in my life hath been
Of what is felt and what is seen—
Sights that do glad the inward ken,
I owe unto the great bard's pen.

For he hath opened to the light
Thoughts that have waked the slumbering sight,
Thoughts that have been through life to me,
The heralds of felicity.

"Churchyard among the mountains" fair,
Sweet resting-place beyond compare;
Peaceful thou art, but still more dear,
Because loved Wordsworth lieth here.

Lightning Source UK Ltd.
Milton Keynes UK
UKHW022225140719
346135UK00003B/31/P